SOUTH AMERICAN MAMMALS

written and illustrated by
JOHN LEIGH-PEMBERTON

Publishers: Ladybird Books Ltd . Loughborough
© Ladybird Books Ltd (formerly Wills & Hepworth Ltd) 1972
Printed in England

Murine Opossum *(above)*	Length, head and body	15 cm.
	Length of tail	20 cm.
Woolly Opossum *(centre)*	Length, head and body	25 cm.
	Length of tail	38 cm.
'Four-eyed' Opossum *(below)*	Length, head and body	30 cm.
	Length of tail	28 cm.

The Marsupial* mammals of America belong to the Opossum family (*Didelphidae*), all but one of which are found exclusively from Mexico to Patagonia. The exception is the North American Opossum which extends as far as Canada. They are found in all sorts of habitats other than high mountains or open plains. They are mostly omnivorous, arboreal and nocturnal; some have typical marsupial pouches and in some the tail is prehensile.

Forty species of Murine (*Mouse*) Opossum are found from Mexico to Argentina in forest habitats or banana plantations. Nests, built of twigs and leaves, or a disused bird's nest are used for shelter. As many as ten young are born at a time, and breeding takes place throughout the year. There is no pouch, but the minute young, born after a gestation period of no more than twelve days, cling to the mother's nipples or to her fur. The tail is prehensile and the eyes reflect deep red in daylight.

The Woolly Opossum lives in forests from Mexico to Ecuador and Brazil and is more diurnal than some other Opossums. The tail is prehensile, but there is no true pouch. In diet, breeding and nest building they are similar to Murine Opossums.

The 'Four-eyed' Opossum, so called because of the light patches above the eyes, occupies the same range and habitat. Less arboreal than other species, and a good swimmer, it is noisier and more aggressive when threatened. The tail is prehensile, and three to eight young are kept in the female's fully formed pouch.

* *See 'Australian Mammals' in this series for an account of other marsupials.*

0 7214 0312 3

To some extent the mammals of South America have developed independently of those of the rest of the world. For until a few million years ago – a short time in the earth's total existence – South America was a huge island. It was unconnected to any other land mass and separated from North America by ocean in which was an archipelago of large islands where today the isthmus of Central America exists.

Even after the continents became joined, the migration of mammals in each direction across the narrow land bridge must have been slow. Many species were unable to adjust to competition from the migrants and became extinct.

This process is still going on. For instance, the Armadillo and the Opossum, both South American species, are gradually moving northwards, and some of the cats, such as the Jaguar and the Ocelot are leaving the north for the south.

But some species, such as the South American monkeys, never migrated at all. This was partly for climatic reasons and partly because great natural barriers, formed by rivers, deserts and high mountain ranges, often tend to confine species to a limited area.

Notice that some well-known families are not represented at all in South America. For example there are no wild cattle or antelopes (BOVIDAE), no apes (PONGIDAE) and no wild horses or asses (EQUIDAE). But this continent, known as the Neotropical Zone, presents a fascinating array of mammals. To this day we know very little about many of them, and there may even now be new species to be discovered.

A Ladybird Book
Series 691

South American Mammals is the sixth of a Ladybird series of books about animals of the world. The superb, full-colour illustrations by John Leigh-Pemberton, the well-known bird and animal painter, are supported by an informative text.

A colourful endpaper shows the various types of habitat of the animals. An index is given and also, at the back of the book, a chart showing the various Orders and Families to which the animals belong.

| **Douroucouli** | Length, head and body | 30 cm. |
| (above left) | Length of tail | 36 cm. |

| **Capuchin Monkey** | Length, head and body | 34 cm. |
| (centre right) | Length of tail | 45 cm. |

| **Squirrel Monkey** | Length, head and body | 32 cm. |
| (below) | Length of tail | 38 cm. |

There are seventy species of Monkeys and Marmosets in South America, representing more than half the total number of anthropoid species for the whole world. They are not closely related to the Old World Monkeys of Asia and Africa, although somewhat similar in appearance and many other respects. South American Monkeys (family *Cebidae*, order *Primates*) do not have cheek pouches or bare rump patches as Old World Monkeys* (family *Cercopithecidae*) do; and some of them have prehensile tails, which are never present in Old World Monkeys. The Cebidae are arboreal and diurnal forest dwellers, chiefly vegetarian, often very noisy and usually producing single offspring.

The Douroucouli or 'Night Ape' is the only monkey which is nocturnal. Found from Nicaragua to northern Argentina, they are notable for the variety of sounds they make. The long tail is not prehensile, but Douroucouli are remarkably agile and adept at catching insects, spiders and even bats.

The Capuchin Monkey is found in two distinct forms – those of the northern part of the range, which have tufts of hair on their heads; and those of the southern type, which are tuftless and often black and white. The tail is slightly prehensile and carried curved inwards. Most of the monkeys kept in captivity belong to this genus (*Cebus*).

Squirrel Monkeys range from Panama to Brazil, living in large bands of up to a hundred members. They are the commonest monkeys in South America. Some individuals are exceptionally long-lived and grow to four times the size of the average adult. The tail is not prehensile.

* See 'African Mammals' and 'Asian Mammals' in this series.

Howler Monkey
(*above*)

| Length, head and body | 75–90 cm. |
| Length of tail | 75–90 cm. |

Red-faced Uakari
(*below*)

| Length, head and body | 55 cm. |
| Length of tail | 16 cm. |

The largest of the South American Monkeys is the Howler, three types of which occur in tropical areas from Mexico to Paraguay and also in Trinidad. Colour varies from yellowish brown to black, but individuals vary and the colour is reputed to fade if washed.

Howlers live in small troupes occupying definite territories which are defended by the use of their astonishingly loud voices, rather in the manner of song-birds. The lower jaw and throat are greatly enlarged to accommodate the special anatomical apparatus required for this activity. These monkeys, which live chiefly in the tops of large trees, have powerfully prehensile tails from which they can hang, leaving both hands and feet free to gather the leaves and fruit upon which they live.

Young are born singly and, as with some other South American monkeys, the gestation period is about a hundred and forty days, somewhat less than that of the Old World Monkeys.

The Sad-faced Uakari occurs along the banks of the Amazon river system in three species, distinguished by colour of hair and facial skin, which can be white, red or black. These quiet, shy animals live in small groups in high trees and are slow and almost clumsy in their movements. When nervous they blush, but are aggressive if their young are threatened.

The short tail is not prehensile and is almost useless as a balancing limb. When walking on their hind legs their pitifully thin bodies become most noticeable. Like Howlers they do not thrive in captivity and all three Uakari species are rare enough to be in some danger of extinction.

Woolly Monkey
(above)

| Length, head and body | 60 cm. |
| Length of tail | 66 cm. |

Spider Monkey
(below)

| Length, head and body | 40–63·5 cm. |
| Length of tail | 50–85 cm. |

Three species of Woolly Monkey are found in forests from Colombia and Ecuador to Peru and Brazil. They have fully prehensile tails, the underside of which is bare near the tip, and live in small groups, often in company with other species such as Capuchins. Although arboreal they are not particularly active and often descend to the ground where they walk upright, propping themselves up with the braced tail and balancing, rather like a tightrope walker, with their arms. The single young is carried by the mother on her back or belly, as is common with most monkeys.

All monkeys make very unsatisfactory pets, but, in the care of experts, Woolly Monkeys, in spite of powerful jaws and massive teeth, have been found to be less unreliable and aggressive and become remarkably affectionate. They are, however, delicate and prone to die in captivity.

There are four species of Spider Monkeys, varying in colour from yellowish to black. The enormously long limbs and fully prehensile tail make this one of the most agile of all monkeys. They occur in tropical forest areas from Mexico to Bolivia, occupying the highest branches of trees through which they travel by swinging in the manner of the Gibbons*. Small groups occupy a definite territory, keeping in touch with each other and with other groups by short, barking noises.

When disturbed they throw dead branches at the intruder. There is no fixed breeding season, the single young, born at any time of the year, being dependent on its mother for the first ten months of its life.

* *See 'Asian Mammals' in this series.*

Golden Lion **Marmoset** (*above*)	Length, head and body (average)	28 cm.
	Length of tail (average)	30 cm.
Silvery Marmoset (*below*)	Length, head and body about	20 cm.
	Length of tail about	25 cm.

There are thirty-three species of Marmosets (family *Callithricidae*) and these are usually divided into two groups – Marmosets and Tamarins, which are distinguished by having longer tusks. These wonderful little creatures are the smallest Primates, the Pygmy Marmoset having a head and body length of fifteen cms. and a weight of some seventy grams. They occur in great variety, in all colours and with plumes, ruffs, moustaches or ear tufts of all kinds. Next to the great Apes* they have the most varied facial expressions of all Primates, ears, lips and eyelids being used to convey their feelings. They use their hands extensively and are scrupulously clean.

One to three young are born at a time in a nest in a hollow tree. The father assists at the birth of his young, taking them from the mother and washing them. He carries them about and hands them to the mother every two or three hours to be fed.

Marmosets are found in the tropical forests of South America, principally in the Amazon region. They live in troupes or family groups and are diurnal and largely arboreal. They utter squeals and bird-like chirps and, like all Primates, are brave and intelligent. They feed mostly on insects and fruit and have highly developed senses of sight, smell and hearing. The tail is not prehensile.

Ever since the discovery of South America by Europeans, thousands of Marmosets have been captured as pets. (Madame de Pompadour owned a Golden Lion Marmoset.) Many of these captives die almost at once, but the trade still continues and today many species have become extremely rare.

* See 'African Mammals' and 'Asian Mammals' in this series.

| **Savannah Fox** | Length, head and body | 65 cm. |
| (*above*) | Length of tail | 30 cm. |

| **Hairy Armadillo** | Length, head and body | 25 cm. |
| (*below*) | Length of tail | 10 cm. |

The Savannah Fox (or Crab-eating Fox) is commonly found in Colombia and Venezuela and also occurs as far south as Argentina. This member of the family *Canidae* enjoys an extremely mixed diet – anything from small rodents to great quantities of insects and fruit and including crabs. It is mainly nocturnal and for most of the year is solitary. At certain times of the year it is said to be prone to rabies. Two to five pups are born in a burrow taken over from some other animal.

There are altogether about twelve species of *Canidae* in South America, most of them inhabiting the grasslands or open woodland and only a few occupying thick jungle habitats. They are found throughout the whole continent.

Armadillos (order *Edentata*, family *Dasypodidae*) are found only in South America and in the south eastern United States where the Nine-banded Armadillo is gradually extending its range. The outer skin is formed into horn-like scales arranged in bands or plates which offer effective protection against predators. Armadillos are chiefly insectivorous but will eat plants or carrion and sometimes kill snakes. They are active by both day and night and are tremendous burrowers, having powerful claws on their forefeet for this purpose.

About twenty species, ranging from the Giant Armadillo of eastern South America to the little 'Fairy' Armadillos of Argentina, are found mostly in savannah country.

The Hairy Armadillo comes from Bolivia and Argentina and occurs even at high altitudes in Peru. It produces two young at a birth, always one male and one female. Other Armadillos habitually produce several pairs of identical twins.

14

| **Two-toed Sloth** (*above*) | Length, head and body | 62 cm. |

| **Tamandua** (*below*) | Length, head and body | 56 cm. |
| | Length of tail | 55 cm. |

The order *Edentata* contains some thirty species of Sloths, Anteaters and Armadillos. All of them are found only in the New World and are very primitive mammals with small brains and unusual anatomical features. Although the word 'Edentate' means 'without teeth' this is true only of the Anteaters, for other members of this order have simple teeth and some Armadillos more teeth than any other land mammal.

Generally speaking *Edentata* are insectivorous, solitary and nocturnal; but some are active during the day and are partially vegetarian.

The Two-toed Sloth is found in forests in northern South America; it belongs to the family *Bradypodidae*, is arboreal and vegetarian, and spends almost its whole life hanging upside down from its strong, hooked claws. It is quite helpless on the ground but can swim well, using a breast stroke much in the manner of humans. All its movements, except when defending itself with its sharp claws, are extremely slow, and its body temperature varies more than that of any other mammal. Moths and algae grow in the fur. The young are produced singly after a very long period of gestation.

The Tamandua, or Lesser Anteater, is an insectivorous and nocturnal member of the family *Myrmecophagidae*, partly arboreal and with a prehensile tail.

These animals have immensely strong arms with which they defend themselves while assuming an upright position, often with the back braced against a tree. Their diet consists of ants, termites and bees. After ripping open the insects' nest, Tamanduas collect them on their long, sticky tongues. They inhabit tropical forest from Mexico to Brazil and produce single young.

Giant Anteater	Length, head and body	110 cm.
(above)	Length of tail	85 cm.
Mara *(below)*	Length, head and body	72 cm.
	Length of tail	4 cm.

The Giant Anteater (order *Edentata*, family *Myrmecop-hagidae*) is found in savannah country and in swamps or forest in Central and South America as far south as northern Argentina. This is the largest of the Edentates, wholly insectivorous, solitary, diurnal and producing single young which are born in the spring and thereafter carried by the mother on her back.

Giant Anteaters walk on the sides of their fore-feet, thereby keeping the claws, used for ripping up ants' nests, long and sharp. These same claws can be used to good effect in defence, the powerful forearms being used to hold an opponent. A sort of ambling walk is the usual gait but Giant Anteaters can gallop if alarmed and are good swimmers. They are usually avoided by predators, even the Jaguar. All food is collected on the long, sticky tongue and drawn into the toothless mouth which is in the form of a tube.

The Mara or Patagonian 'Hare' belongs to the family *Caviidae*, order *Rodentia*, which also includes the Cavies or 'Guinea Pigs'. It inhabits pampas country from Argentina to Patagonia.

Maras dig burrows like rabbits do. They are diurnal, spending much time lying (more like a dog or cat than a rodent) in the sun. They are vegetarian and usually live in small groups. Two to five young are born in each of two litters every year. The mother feeds her young in a sitting position.

In spite of their long legs and hare-like appearance, Maras are not particularly fast runners. They are becoming scarce since the introduction into their habitat of the European Hare.

Chinchilla (*above*)	Length, head and body	30 cm.
	Length of tail	12 cm.
Leaf-eared Mouse	Length, head and body	12 cm.
	Length of tail	11 cm.
(*below*)	Length of ears	3 cm.

An enormous number of rodent species is found in South America, many of them very large and most of them quite unlike the rodents found anywhere else. They occupy every type of habitat, extending into the high plateaux of the Andes or the swamps and rivers of the dense forest of Brazil.

The Chinchilla (family *Chinchillidae*) occurs in two species, the short-tailed of Argentina, Bolivia and Peru which is practically extinct in the wild, and the long-tailed (shown here) which is found in Chile and Bolivia. Both species inhabit rocky areas in the Andes Mountains and have been ruthlessly hunted for their beautiful fur. Many are kept on fur farms and those left in the wild are now protected by law.

Chinchillas are gregarious, vegetarian, principally nocturnal and they mate for life. One to three litters, each of up to six young, are produced each year. They have been introduced into Tajikistan in southern U.S.S.R., where they are said to be flourishing.

Several other rodents, such as Mountain Viscachas (not shown) also inhabit mountain areas. Among them are the little Leaf-eared Mice (family *Cricetidae*), often found in company with other rodents. They occur in about fifteen species, some nocturnal, others diurnal, found in savannah country as well as mountains. They eat seeds, vegetation and lichens and produce two litters each year of three or four young.

Sometimes called 'Pericotes', these mice take the place, in their South American habitat, of the very similar Deer Mice* (White-footed Mice) of North America. Their range extends all the way from Ecuador to Patagonia.

* See 'North American Mammals' in this series.

Dwarf Neotropical Squirrel (*above*)	*Length, head and body*	15 cm.
	Length of tail	14 cm.
Kinkajou (*centre*)	*Length, head and body*	50 cm.
	Length of tail	50 cm.
Prehensile-tailed Porcupine (*below*)	*Length, head and body*	45 cm.
	Length of tail	40 cm.

Squirrels are well represented in South America, among them the seventeen species of Dwarf Neotropical Squirrels (family *Sciuridae*) which range from Nicaragua to Peru. They occur in woodland and in hilly palm forest and probably provide a food source for many bird and mammal predators. They have not been extensively studied but seem to be similar in breeding and other habits to the Squirrels of North America*.

Kinkajous belong to the family *Procyonidae*. These forest animals are found from Mexico to the Mato Grosso in Brazil. They are entirely arboreal, having a prehensile tail, and although classed as *Carnivora* their diet consists very largely of fruit. They are nocturnal, moving carefully about in the trees and occasionally uttering a shrill scream which can be heard a kilometre away.

Young are usually born singly, but twins occur. At seven weeks old they can hang by their tails. For so small an animal they are surprisingly long lived – about twenty years. A somewhat similar animal (but with a non-prehensile tail) occurs in the same habitat; it is known as the Olingo (see title page).

Prehensile-tailed Porcupines grasp a branch with the upper side of their tails, the gripping surface being so placed and not underneath as is commonly the case. These rodents (family *Erethizontidae*) live in forests from Mexico to Brazil. Nocturnal, arboreal, slow moving but sure-footed, they live on leaves and fruit and produce single young which, as with all Porcupines*, are highly developed at birth.

These animals, which have a strong smell, are aggressive if attacked and their spines are sharp and barbed.

* *See 'North American Mammals' in this series.*

Capybara (*above*)	Length, head and body	120 cm.
	Shoulder height	50 cm.
Guira (*centre*)	Length, head and body	22 cm.
	Length of tail	5 cm.
Coypu (*below*)	Length, head and body	60 cm.
	Length of tail	37 cm.

The largest rodent in the world is the Capybara (family *Hydrochoeridae*) which frequents wooded areas close to streams, rivers and swamps. Groups of up to twenty individuals are active at dawn and dusk, but in areas of human settlement they tend, as some other normally diurnal mammals do, to become entirely nocturnal. They lead semi-aquatic lives and all four feet are partly webbed.

These are quiet, rather dignified animals, entirely vegetarian and a little more intelligent than most rodents. They are hunted by Jaguars, by Alligators and by Man. Two to eight young are born in one litter each year. They are found from Panama to Argentina.

Guiras are found in grass country, chiefly in wet areas of Brazil. They belong to the family *Echimyidae*, the Spiny Rats, most of whom have stiff, pointed hairs mixed in their fur. They are vegetarian, nocturnal and about the size of the common Brown Rat*. They produce two litters each year of about three young. There are seventy-two species of Spiny Rats and in some parts of South America they are the commonest mammal.

Coypus (or Nutria) belong to the rodent family *Capromyidae* and are semi-aquatic animals which live in tidal waters as well as swamps, lakes and rivers. They are found in the central parts of South America and, because of their fur, have been introduced into the United States and into many countries of Europe where they have become a destructive pest. They eat shellfish as well as plant food and produce up to nine young which can themselves breed at five months.

* *See 'European Mammals' in this series.*

Tayra (*above*)	Length, head and body	65 cm.
	Length of tail	40 cm.
Bush Dog (*below*)	Length, head and body	65 cm.
	Length of tail	13 cm.

The Tayra (order *Carnivora*, family *Mustelidae*) is a fairly large, graceful equivalent in South America of the Fisher* in North America. These relatives of the Marten are found in forest country from Mexico to Argentina and in Trinidad. In places they are quite common and are active by both day and night. They tend to live in pairs or in family groups and prey on small mammals and birds. They also eat honey and fruit and are said to be particularly fond of bananas.

Tayras are good swimmers and also climb and run well. They make nests in hollow trees where from two to four young are born each year. Like other members of this family they possess glands which can emit a powerful scent, said to be less offensive than in other *Mustelidae*.

The curious Bush Dog (family *Canidae*) is a little-known carnivore which looks like a short-legged terrier. It occurs in dense vegetation in forest areas of Central and South America and is nocturnal. Because of this and also because it is undoubtedly a rare animal it is not often seen and little is known about it.

Bush Dogs produce three or four pups in a litter and often live in the abandoned burrows of Armadillos. They hunt in packs, the prey consisting mainly of rodents, and whine and bark like a dog. They are intelligent and, in captivity, have been found to swim well and, most abnormally for the *Canidae*, to dive and swim under water. Another curious feature is that their facial expressions seem to differ from those of other *Canidae*.

* See 'North American Mammals' in this series.

| **Giant Otter (Saro)** | Length, head and body | 150 cm. |
| (*above*) | Length of tail | 70 cm. |

| **Yapok (Water** | Length, head and body | 30 cm. |
| **Opossum)** (*below*) | Length of tail | 36 cm. |

The Giant Otter, or Saro, is also known as the Flat-tailed or Margin-tailed Otter, due to the flattened tail which has ribbed edges. This is the largest of the *Mustelidae*, found in slow-moving streams of the big river systems of South America. It is entirely aquatic, all feet being heavily webbed and the legs so short as to give the animal the appearance of a seal when on land.

Saros, active in daytime, feed principally on fish, although waterfowl and their eggs are also eaten. They nest in dens on river banks and communicate with each other by means of high-pitched screams. One or two young constitute a litter.

The fur of these animals is of great value and in consequence they have been gravely over-hunted; in some parts of their range they have become very scarce or even extinct.

The Yapok (family *Didelphidae*) is the only truly aquatic marsupial and is found in mountain streams or in lakes from Mexico to Argentina. It is not a common animal and, being nocturnal, is rarely seen.

Fish, shrimps and some vegetation are eaten and, as this animal can also climb and has a partially prehensile tail, it is probable that it also eats fruit. Both sexes have a waterproof pouch and webbed feet. The young, from one to five in a litter, stay in the pouch even when the mother is under water.

As with many other South American mammals, the nocturnal life and inaccessible habitat of the Yapok has made it difficult to study.

Maned Wolf (*above*)	Length, head and body	125 cm.
	Length of tail	30 cm.
	Shoulder height	75 cm.
Small-eared Dog (*below*)	Length, head and body	85 cm.
	Length of tail	30 cm.
	Shoulder height	36 cm.

About thirteen species of Fox-like mammals occur in South America, some being pampas animals and others forest dwellers. Because of their general appearance some of them have been referred to as 'Dogs' or 'Wolves', but most of them have been placed in a separate genus (*Dusicyon*) of the family *Canidae* and others as separate species in a genus of their own.

Thus, the Maned Wolf is the only species in the genus *Chrysocyon*. This elegant animal is found in pampas or wooded country throughout central South America, but it is secretive, solitary and nocturnal and, as it becomes rarer, is not often seen.

Their immensely long legs make it easier for Maned Wolves to travel in areas of long grass and also to run, at least over short distances, at great speed. They live on a diet of rodents, small deer, insects and fruit and produce twin pups once a year. Unlike other *Canidae*, they never dig with their claws but with their teeth.

Even more curious is the Small-eared Dog, also placed in a genus (*Atelocynus*) by itself. This animal, which occurs in the tropical forest of the Amazon basin, has anatomical features which separate it completely from other *Canidae*. It moves through thick vegetation in the manner of a cat and presumably lives on rodents and vegetable matter. But it has been studied only in captivity. Under these circumstances behaviour, diet and breeding habits can become greatly altered, and in fact little is as yet known about *Atelocynus*, as is the case with many other mammals from this region.

Coati (*above*)

Length, head and body
about 60 cm.
Length of tail   about 60 cm.

Grison (*below*)

Length, head and body   50 cm.
Length of tail   16 cm.

Three species of Coati (order *Carnivora*, family *Procyonidae*) occur from south western United States throughout South America. They are usually found in wooded areas living in groups of about ten females and young, the adult males living singly and being known as Coatimundis. They are both nocturnal and diurnal and are omnivorous, using their sensitive, mobile snouts to search for food. They are good climbers, using their long, semi-prehensile tails as a balance.

Coatis are inquisitive and, when cornered, aggressive, being a match for most dogs and using their long, front claws and formidable canine teeth very effectively. The young, from two to six, are born in a specially built tree nest after a gestation period of seventy-seven days. Coatis have been kept as pets but are extraordinarily destructive, as is the case with all the *Procyonidae*.

The Grison occurs in two species, the larger from Mexico to Brazil and Peru and the Little Grison in mountain country throughout central and southern South America. These carnivores are members of the family *Mustelidae*, living in groups and hunting by day and night. They normally live in the burrows of other animals and are good climbers and swimmers, almost entirely carnivorous with a preference for small rodents and birds. From two to four young are born in a litter.

At one time Grisons were used, in the manner of Ferrets, to search out Chinchillas for fur hunters, but this practice is no longer legal. They are often kept as pets in South America and are said to be affectionate and to bark like little dogs.

32

Jaguar

Length, head and body	175 cm.
Length of tail	80 cm.
Shoulder height	85 cm.

Like the Leopard*, the Jaguar is classed as one of the so-called 'Big Cats' – the genus *Panthera* of the family *Felidae*. These two carnivores are somewhat alike, but Jaguars are stockier and less graceful than Leopards and their rosettes of spots contain a central spot, a feature which is absent in the Leopard.

Jaguars are found only in America, from the south western United States, through Central America and from there south-easterly as far as northern Patagonia. Although sometimes seen on the pampas, they are more often found in forests, particularly near water. Such a variety of habitat and occupation of such an extensive range results in the Jaguar occurring in various forms, sizes and colours, and having alternative names such as 'El Tigre' or 'Jaguare'.

Deer, rodents and Peccaries form the principal diet, but alligators and fish are taken from streams, and Jaguars prey on domestic cattle and are powerful enough to tackle a heavy animal like a Tapir. They usually lie in wait for their prey and catch it in a single bound. They rarely climb trees but, more than most cats, they readily take to the water. Like other members of their genus they can roar and also utter loud, rythmical grunting sounds, rather as Leopards do.

The gestation period for Jaguars is about one hundred days, at the end of which from two to four cubs are born, very dark in colour and with little separation between the spots of their fur. The father takes no part in rearing his young. Breeding takes place at any time of the year.

* See 'African Mammals' in this series.

Ocelot (*above*)	Length, head and body	95 cm.
	Length of tail	30 cm.
Agouti (*below*)	Length, head and body	38 cm.

The Ocelot is the largest of a number of species of small cats found in South America. These include the very similar Margay and Tiger Cats, the Andean Cat of the mountains of Chile and Peru, the Kod-Kod from the Chilean woodlands and Geoffroy's Cat from Argentina.

Ocelots (family *Felidae*) inhabit forests of Central and South America and are normally diurnal, although, like many mammals, they become nocturnal when molested by Man. They live on small deer and many species of rodent as well as a few birds and even snakes.

Most of the Ocelot's life is spent among dense vegetation on the ground, but it can climb well, often lying-up in thick foliage in a tree. The usual litter is of two rather dark cubs.

Unfortunately the fur of Ocelots is extremely fashionable and therefore valuable; and this has resulted in a decrease in their numbers over part of their range, particularly in the United States.

The Agouti (family *Dasyproctidae*) is a common rodent found from Mexico to southern Brazil and occurring in about twenty-four species among which there is great variety of coloration. Long legs and little hoof-like claws on each foot give this animal almost the appearance of a small antelope.

Agoutis are diurnal, vegetarian and usually solitary, occupying differing types of habitat. They are exceptionally nervous, either 'freezing' or rushing about in panic if threatened. They are extensively preyed upon by predators and hunted, for food, by Man.

Two litters of from two to four young are born in a burrow which contains a grassy nest.

Jaguarundi (*above*)	Length, head and body	75 cm.
	Length of tail	45 cm.
	Shoulder height	30 cm.

| **Hog-nosed Skunk** | Length, head and body | 40 cm. |
| (*below*) | Length of tail | 32 cm. |

Of all the family *Felidae* the Jaguarundi is the least cat-like. Extremely short legs, small ears and a weasel-like head give it the appearance of an Otter, and indeed in Mexico it is known as the "Otter-cat". It ranges from the south-western United States to Paraguay and inhabits wooded areas near streams. It is a particularly good swimmer and, in spite of its short legs, hunts by running after its prey. This consists of small mammals and particularly of birds, but the Jaguarundi will also eat fruit for which it will climb into trees.

This species is found in two colour phases, grey and red, both of which can occur in the same litter. At one time it was thought that the red coloured animals constituted a separate species known as the *Eyra*. From two to four cubs are born in a litter and in some areas there may be two litters a year, the cubs being only faintly spotted.

Jaguarundis are active by day and night and, except during the mating period in November, are solitary.

Hog-nosed Skunks (family *Mustelidae*) are found in about six species from the southern United States, where they overlap the North American species*, to the Strait of Magellan. Unlike the northern species they have no white stripe down the centre of the face and their noses are broad and hairless. They are in other respects similar to the northern species in behaviour and breeding habits. They appear to be impervious to snake venom, and snakes, including rattlesnakes, are included in their omnivorous diet.

* *See 'North American Mammals' in this series.*

Pudu (*above*)

Length, head and body	80 cm.
Length of tail	4 cm.
Shoulder height	40 cm.

Pampas Cat (*below*)

Length, head and body	75 cm.
Length of tail	25 cm.

The Pudu (family *Cervidae*, order *Artiodactyla*) occurs in two species; one, shown here, is found in Chile and Bolivia and possibly on some islands off the Chilean coast. The other, which is much smaller, occurs in Ecuador. Both species are rare in parts of their range and are forest dwellers on the slopes of the Andes mountains. These are the smallest American deer, very shy and not often seen. They are now protected in a National Park but were previously hunted by being driven by dogs into the sea and there picked up by men in boats.

Fawns of Pudu are spotted and although they are easily tamed they generally do not thrive in captivity when adult, the males in particular becoming desperate and often dying from exhaustion. However, there are accounts of these little deer being kept, like dogs, in houses.

The Pampas Cat (family *Felidae*) is yet another of the small and almost unknown carnivores of South America. It has a large range, being at one time found in Uruguay and Argentina and possibly in Chile, not only in pampas country but also in reed beds. Due to human development in its former territory it is becoming extremely scarce and has probably been driven into more inaccessible habitats.

The Pampas Cat is a nocturnal hunter of birds and small mammals, especially 'Guinea Pigs' and young Vicunas. It produces two or three kittens in a litter. Like some other small cats of South America who share roughly the same range, Pampas Cats are rarely seen in the wild and even less frequently in zoos.

| **Andean Deer** | Length, head and body | 150 cm. |
| **(Guemal)** (*above*) | Length of tail | 12 cm. |

Spectacled Bear	Length, head and body	175 cm.
	Length of tail	7 cm.
(*below*)	Shoulder height	75 cm.

There are two species of Andean Deer, or Guemals, one in southern Chile and Patagonia, and the other (shown here) in Peru, Ecuador and Bolivia. These members of the family *Cervidae* inhabit the grassy hills and forests of the Andes Mountains and occur at altitudes of up to five thousand metres. Only the males have the simple antlers but both sexes possess tusk-like, canine teeth similar to those of the Musk Deer and Chinese Water Deer of Asia*.

These rather short-legged deer lie up during the day but are active at dusk, feeding in small groups on lichens and moss as well as other vegetation. Breeding habits are the same as for other members of this family, which is represented in South America by some eighteen species.

The Spectacled Bear (order *Carnivora*, family *Ursidae*) is the only bear found in South America or indeed in the southern hemisphere. This fairly small bear lives in mountainous regions from Venezuela and Ecuador to Peru and Bolivia. It is not a common animal although often kept in zoos, and is solitary and far more vegetarian than most of this family. However, it is said to prey on such animals as deer and Vicunas, and its diet is probably dictated by the time of year, the availability of food and the tastes of individual bears.

One to three cubs are born in a litter and, as with all bears, they are very small but grow rapidly. Spectacled Bears are said to make large sleeping nests, built of sticks, in trees. This is a most unusual activity for a carnivore.

* See 'Asian Mammals' in this series.

42

Swamp Deer	Length, head and body	
(*above left, hind and stag*)		up to 200 cm.
	Shoulder height	up to 110 cm.

Brocket Deer	Length, head and body	
(*above right*)		up to 120 cm.
	Shoulder height	up to 65 cm.

Brazilian Tapir	Length, head and body	185 cm.
(*below*)	Length of tail	8 cm.
	Shoulder height	98 cm.

From the Guianas, through Brazil to Uruguay, Swamp Deer and Brocket Deer are found in damp forest areas with plenty of cover. The deer of open country is the Pampas Deer (not shown), a marvellously athletic animal which is in grave danger of extinction.

Swamp Deer feed largely on aquatic plants and spend much time in the water. They are the largest of the South American deer with the biggest and most complex antlers. These are shed at varying times of the year and, unlike most other *Cervidae*, there is no definite breeding season, the single young being born at any season. This breeding habit occurs most often in animals of a tropical habitat where food supplies are abundant throughout the year.

The timid, rarely seen Brocket Deer occur in about ten species. They are diurnal and live singly or in pairs. They are greatly preyed upon by carnivores and snakes and seem to have inadequate means of defence or escape. Breeding is much the same as for Swamp Deer.

The three species of Tapir (order *Perissodactyla*, family *Tapiridae*) found in Central and South America are closely related to the Malayan Tapir of Asia*. One species occurs in mountain country but all prefer a wooded habitat near water.

Tapirs are vegetarian, solitary and, considering their bulk, extremely active both on land and in water. They create paths through the densest undergrowth and can walk, like Hippos, under water. They breed at any time of the year, producing one or two young after a gestation period of as much as four hundred days.

* *See 'Asian Mammals' in this series.*

Llama (*above*)	Length, head and body	120 cm.
	Length of tail	15 cm.
	Shoulder height	120 cm.
Guanaco (*below*)	Length, head and body	150 cm.
	Length of tail	25 cm.
	Shoulder height	120 cm.

The six species of the family *Camelidae* (order *Artiodactyla*) evolved from a small, common ancestor in North America. From here some spread to Asia* and Africa* across the land bridge that once spanned the Bering Strait and survive today as the humped camels of those regions. Others migrated to South America where today four species exist. The original North American stock failed to survive.

The South American camels are animals of the high desert regions, able to exist at elevations of five thousand metres. They do not have humps, but have the split upper lip, the double row of lashes, the ambling gait and other features typical of this family. *Camelidae* have red blood corpuscles which are different from those of all other mammals, for they are oval, as in birds, rather than round.

Llamas exist today only in a domesticated form, and have been so since the days of the Inca civilization. They are a most important animal to the Peruvian Indian, providing him with wool and meat, leather and even fuel (from the droppings). Moreover, the Llama is a superb beast of burden, able to carry unlimited loads at altitudes which no other animal could stand.

The Guanaco is a wild species inhabiting high, grassy plains in the Andes from Peru to Tierra del Fuego. It is the tallest of the wild South American mammals, living in small herds of two kinds, one, led by a male, consisting of females, and the other of young males.

All this family can bite and spit if annoyed, and the Guanaco is probably the most aggressive of them all.

* See 'Asian Mammals' and 'African Mammals' in this series.

Alpaca (*above*)	Length, head and body	120 cm.
	Length of tail	15 cm.
	Shoulder height	109 cm.
Vicuna (*below*)	Length, head and body	140 cm.
	Length of tail	15 cm.
	Shoulder height	78 cm.

Since the fourth century B.C. the Alpaca has been kept in domesticated herds entirely for its wool. It does not exist in the wild state and occurs in a variety of colours, black and brown being the commonest and white the most valued. Alpacas live all the year round on grassland at very high altitudes, particularly in the region of Lake Titicaca, and are rounded up every two years for shearing.

Like the other *Camelidae*, Alpacas produce single young (rarely twins). They have been crossed with Llamas and also with Vicunas in order to produce a finer fleece.

The Vicuna is the smallest and by far the lightest of the *Camelidae*, and much of its total length is made up of its extra long neck. It is a delicate, graceful animal living on coarse grasses in the very highest mountains up to almost six thousand metres in the Andes from Peru to central Chile. Vicunas are preyed upon by foxes and various cats but can run very swiftly and have exceptional eyesight.

The finest wool in the world is produced by these animals and, although a wild species, they are rounded up and shorn by the Indians. Because of the great value of the wool they have been much hunted by poachers who shoot them instead of shearing them and then releasing them; it has therefore been found necessary to protect them. But in so large an area it is difficult to enforce protective laws and, as long as the export of Vicuna wool continues, the Vicuna is in some danger of a drastic decrease in numbers.

Puma (*above*)

Length, head and body	150 cm.
Length of tail	75 cm.

Collared Peccary
(*below*)

Length, head and body	80 cm.
Shoulder height	45 cm.

The Puma* occurs from Canada and the United States through Mexico and Central America and from there down South America to Patagonia. It is rare in the tropical forests of Brazil, which is 'Jaguar country', and the jungle types seem to be smaller and darker in colour than those found on the open pampas. On the whole, the Pumas of South America tend to be smaller than those of North America. It is nevertheless one of the principal predators of South America, preying upon other mammals from the larger rodents to deer, Peccaries, Vicunas and even, in Patagonia, on sea-lions.

Because it preyed upon Vicunas and Llamas and, latterly on sheep, the Puma has always been ruthlessly hunted in South America ever since Inca times.

There are two species of Peccary (order *Artiodactyla*, family *Tayassuidae*) found in Texas and in Central and South America. These are the Collared Peccary, seen here, so called because of the pale, coloured band round the shoulders, and the White-lipped Peccary of damp forests. Both collect in herds – the Collared Peccary, which is a desert or woodland animal, of about ten animals, and the White-lipped in herds of as many as a hundred. When angry they can be very dangerous.

Principally nocturnal, Peccaries are omnivorous. The number of young is usually two and these are not striped as those of the pigs are.

Although somewhat pig-like in appearance, Peccaries are not very closely related to pigs, differing from them in many respects, including the possession of a musk gland on the back and small tusks in both jaws.

* See 'North American Mammals' in this series.

INDEX